Through the Eyes of a Failure

Patrick Murphy

Through the Eyes of a Failure

How to Succeed When You Feel Like Giving Up

Patrick Murphy

Library of Congress Control Number: 2016916291

CreateSpace Independent Publishing Platform

North Charleston, South Carolina

Contents

The Mind
and its Harmful Partner

*I*t is absolutely amazing to me how the mind works. It has such power. Our minds can create the most fascinating and beautiful objects the world has ever seen. It can also create sinister objects that destroy entire nations. Our minds can be filled with love for another person, then turn and harbor bitterness, anger, and resentment towards that very same person. Our minds tell us stories. And whether those stories are true or not, the mind does not always filter information to ensure that it processes "truth" only. The mind takes journeys through time and space. It can travel to unknown worlds of its own formation. Our minds can be used to help ourselves and others, or they can be used to harm ourselves and others. One would think that the mind would do all it can to preserve the vessel that houses it, but that is not the case. Often times, the possessor of such a magnificent tool is decayed by the tool itself. The funny thing is this, the possessor of the mind may not recognize the destruction the mind is causing to him or her. The very thing responsible for reminding your body to take its next breath also causes many to decide to take their last. One moment, your mind keeps you safe, by telling you to breathe, or blink, or swallow, but the next, it may end it all by deciding that suicide is the only answer. The mind, which humans can utilize in such unique ways, often uses it to destroy him or herself.

How could this be? How could one with such power mismanage such a magnificent instrument as the mind? There lies the question that will be answered in the following pages. We will explore the Power of our Will, and discover how it acts as the driving force for the vehicle called the mind. We will see how we initiate our own success or failure through the power of our will and mind. Had we been created without a will, our minds could have simply been pre-programmed to perform a certain way with no deviation. But, through our will, our minds can program themselves and thus create our world from our own thoughts. The mind and will have the power, on a small scale, to act as God. They can create from thought alone.

Over the course of this book, we will take a look at how I fared with my own mental tools. We'll see how my will steered my mind, how my mind sought to protect itself, or not, and what my will and my mind created.

The Dreamer

My dream was to be married, successful, and wealthy. I don't know where this desire came from, but it has always lived inside of me. My dream was to become someone of importance. I wanted to be someone of significance who could touch lives all over the world with his voice. Even though I was a religious man, I had no desire to be a preacher. I wanted to be a motivational speaker. Looking back now, maybe I should have become a preacher. I like preaching, but didn't want the responsibilities that came with that platform. I wanted to stand on stages around the world, speaking to people about all the life-lessons I had learned over the course of my journey. I had no desire to be a senator or the President of the United States. I simply wanted to motivate people to handle the challenges we all face in our day-to-day lives. I also wanted wealth and abundance as I toured the world helping others. It is nice to want to save the world, but it's hard to do so when you are broke and in need of help yourself. I knew I was meant to be more than average, but trying and failing only mocked this dreamer. To me, being a dreamer is torturous. Before granting you anything, Life will put you in its boxing ring and it will punch away at you to see if you deserve what you are seeking from it. To have a desire or aspiration is to invite pain into your life. Dreams cost.

I remember starting out as a grown man, if that's what you would call me at eighteen years old, having big dreams in my heart that were in direct contrast to my reality. For example, my first marriage didn't start with what you would call a dream wedding. We didn't have money for a traditional ceremony, so we got creative. It was a sunny, Saturday afternoon. We arrived at the church dressed like we were going to a friend's home for a barbeque. She had on a nice blue sweater and a short blue jean skirt. I had on a grey, spotted sweater with matching grey overalls. Don't laugh. That was the style back then. As to why we had on sweaters on a warm California afternoon would be anybody's guess. My eldest brother Jimmy and his wife Vickie were our best man, maid of honor, and witnesses all rolled into one.

We arrived at the church on time, but even then we each secretly feared that we were not meant to be together. The pastor's tardiness did not help to ease our fears. As we were waiting at the locked door of the church, our anxieties tried to convince us that the pastor's lateness was a sign from God. We toyed with the idea of going home and continuing what the church people called "Shacking." The term "Shacking" meant that you were living together but not married. However, as we were walking to our car, the pastor flung the church door open and called to us, "Ha, where are you guys going?" We looked at each other and proceeded towards the smiling pastor. The pastor appeared to be happier to be there than we were.

Moments after we entered the church, we were married. It takes longer to get a pizza delivered than it did to attend our elaborate wedding. Now, the reception was one for the record books. We left the church and went down a few blocks to our extravagant location, a little restaurant called Wendy's. That's right, the hamburger joint. She ordered the #1, and I had the #4. It was our wedding day, so, of course, everything was supersized. After the elaborate reception, we walked out ready to begin our lives as a power couple.

However, things didn't start out so strong. Some of you may remember several years ago when the government used to hand out free butter and cheese; that long yellow brick of processed cheese. Back then, I was so financially challenged (broke) that I had no choice but to depend on these items to feed my family. I stood in line outside the government building in downtown Oakland waiting my turn to receive my government gifts. I recall telling myself, "I do not belong here." As I marched along in single file waiting to be served, I thought to myself, "One day, I will never need to come back to this humiliating line again." That was my dream.

Our first place together was at my dad's rental property, which we shared with my sister Leslie. It was a two-bedroom home; we occupied one of the bedrooms while my sister resided in the other. We enjoyed the family atmosphere, but as newlyweds, we needed to find a place of our own. Our first apartment was a studio that we rented from my wife's grand-parents. It was cute. As soon as you opened the front door, you were standing in our living room/bedroom. The view from the front door introduced you to the entire apartment. The bathroom was two feet from the front door. Then there was a small hallway which lead to a surprisingly large kitchen; it was bigger than our entire living quarters. The place was small, but it was ours. In fact, our unit was built as a home for the live-in maintenance guy, which I later became.

I remember spending our weekends going to neighborhoods where new homes were being built. We would visit model homes by different developers and dream of having a larger place to live. It's hard to dream of a big home when you're broke, but dream we did. As my dad use to say, "you have champagne dreams with Kool-Aid money." I recall watching a show on television called, *MTV Cribs*. The idea behind the show was to take the viewer on a tour of the way celebrities and other rich people lived. They typically showcased the homes of famous sport stars and actors. Everyone I knew loved to watch that show. But me, I hated it. Every episode would bring me to tears. You might think that was strange behavior, but for me, those shows were not entertainment. Those shows mocked the dreamer in me. I was not being covetous of those who had obtained their dreams, but I longed to know where mine was. It was difficult to watch someone else living their dream life while mines were nowhere to be found.

One holiday, we were invited to a party at a friend's home. It was our first time at his house, and as I walked through the front door my jaw hit the floor. I had never been in such a large home before. It was like walking into the White House as far as I was concerned. His home was extraordinarily large. There were so many doors! "Wow..." was all that ran through my mind. To this day, I do not remember what was served or who else was there, but I still see that home clearly in my mind. It was not just some *MTV Cribs* home on television; it was real, and I was actually standing inside it. The emotions were overwhelming. In that moment, I said to myself, "One day. One day." That was my next dream.

Our next place was a two-bedroom apartment that we obtained through a government program called "Section 8." Section 8, provided housing assistance to low income families. Boy, did we qualify for that. We made that tiny place as cozy as possible, but it was not in the best of neighborhoods. Still, moving from a maintenance man's accommodations to a two bedroom apartment was an upgrade. It was there that we began raising our family. We had our first two children in that place.

One day, opportunity came knocking at our door. We found out that Habitat for Humanity was accepting applications for low income families who wanted a brand-new starter home. Well, seeing that I was still just a step above the poverty line, I applied.

Who would have guessed that they would actually call and interview us? We were a match! However, there was a small catch. You had to contribute 500 work hours, laboring alongside professional contractors, not only to build your own home, but to build the homes of your future neighbors. That was your down payment. After being accepted into the program, I don't remember my feet touching the ground. I know I must have flown up to heaven and kissed God on the cheek, or maybe He came down and kissed ours. The location was not exactly in the best neighborhoods, but it was in a gated community. That helped us feel safe for us and for our children. I worked very hard and very quickly through my down payment hours. It was endlessly rewarding building our own home and the homes of my soon to be neighbors. To this day, I am grateful to Habitat for Humanity for the start they gave us and the lessons the program taught me.

Our new house didn't take long to complete, and we were excited about preparing for move-in day. For all our neighbors who happened to complete their homes before us, the move-in process was quiet and easy. Ours was anything but. To this day, I don't know why, but the Mayor of Oakland and several television stations came out and did a live televised event for us. Several city officials came along to watch the Mayor present us with the key to our new home. They had a special banner made with our names on it and had it placed across the entire front of our new home. It was amazing. I know for sure that God came down and kissed us this time. We lived there for several years, enjoying the pleasures of being homeowners. Our house may not have been as large as our friend's, but it was ours, and we were proud of it and grateful to have it.

At our local church, Acts Full Gospel, I was allowed to teach in the youth department. I loved teaching my students. All in all, my life seemed to be headed in the right direction. I did not necessarily preach to the kids, but I coached them in the ways of life and taught them how God wanted them to live according to the Bible.

Those Sunday school lessons bled into my day to day life, and I developed an obsession with finding out why it was okay to celebrate Halloween in schools, but not Christmas. I wanted to know why it was just fine that students wore Halloween costumes to class, but celebrating the birth of Christ was against the rules. Kids were not allowed to have the name Jesus anywhere in the schools. Stores began replacing Christmas signs with X-mas signs. I didn't know why, but I was drawn to the issue. I guess God didn't like that His holiday was being cast aside, and He decided to use me as His spokesman. I didn't choose the cause; He chose me.

I researched the subject for quite a long time, then, finally, I presented my findings to my pastor, Dr. Bob Jackson. He was so impressed with my work that he asked me to speak to the entire congregation about the subject. I was in shock. All I could think was, "Are you kidding me? Pat Murphy speaking to hundreds of people?" I had given life a right hook. I was winning the fight. The opportunity presented itself annually for the next several years. Right before Halloween, Pat

Murphy would be the keynote speaker at Acts Full Gospel church. Can you believe it? My first speaking opportunity just like I dreamed several years ago. What made it more special was that my young family could look at their husband and dad on stage, and they could see me attempting to achieve one of my lifelong goals. There is nothing like accomplishing your dreams with your family by your side.

Fast forward a few more years, and things begin to change. Inside our gated community was like an oasis of peace. Right outside the gates, however, individuals were moving in who had, what I would call, "undesirable behaviors." Crime increased dramatically. It wasn't long before our oasis was starting to feel more like the desert.

It was around that time that I bought my first motorcycle. It was painted with The Lakers' yellow and purple, my favorite basketball team at that time. I liked the Golden State Warriors as well, but the Laker colors looked better on my bike. Not long after I got it, I woke up to find that my cherished dream machine had been stolen. We never could figure out how they got through the gate and got the bike out without ever starting it up. I drove for hours through the neighborhood searching for my bike. I asked anyone and everyone I saw walking down the street if they had seen my bike, but I had forgot the neighborhood rule. In the hood, no one snitches. I was angry and out of luck. It was time to move. Just when I was finally feeling comfortable with life, life fought back. It gave my happiness a quick jab and was winning again.

My Failed Attempts
at Success

I made several attempts at becoming rich and successful before we moved out of our Habit for Humanity home. I ran a small restaurant, but let's just say, the area where it was located was not conducive to massive growth. That was my first failed attempt. I tried my hand at operating a daycare, and I had plenty of clients. However, if the clients do not pay, then it's not a daycare; you're just a glorified babysitter. I had no choice but to quit and call the daycare another failed attempt.

Communication has always been my strongest skill, so I tried to use that skill by joining numerous network marketing businesses I thought showed promise. Sadly, my enthusiasm diminished once I had spoken to everyone I knew about the company's products and services, and I still wasn't seeing the growth in my business that I thought I would. I wasn't seeing the same progress that the people on stage receiving rewards and accolades were. Several attempts at network marketing had to be chalked up to several more failures.

At one point, I was a wedding coordinator, and a very good one at that. However, I never mustered up enough desire to do it full time. So instead, I did it as a favor for friends and family. I tried to become a day trader in the stock market, but I lost much more than I ever made. I tried buying and reselling cars, but I found the profit margins too slim to keep the business running. The failed attempts kept stacking up. As the birthdays passed and my circumstances did not change, my dreams grew dimmer and dimmer.

The Big Turn Around

As we were growing up, my dad used to talk to my brothers and sisters and I about real estate. He had big dreams about growing a huge real estate portfolio. My parents owned the house we lived in as well as the house next door. When I was little, I used to see people move in and out of the house next door from time to time, but I never realized that they were my dad's tenants. At one point, he confided in us his dream of buying each one of his children a home as a graduation present. As wonderful as that would have been, for whatever reason, he was unable to fulfill that dream. He was only ever able to obtain the house next door, not much of a portfolio.

I guess I caught the real estate fever from my dad. I went to school and became a licensed real estate agent. Funny thing is, I never sold a single property as an agent. However, I did receive a big break when our grandmother sold us the four-unit apartment building that we used to live in. Remember maintenance man's apartment with the bedroom two feet away from the front door? Yep, that's the one. Not only were we going to be the proud owners of that unit, but the other three larger adjacent units as well. Can you image that? My first rental property! After purchasing the building, we managed to take out a loan on that property to use to purchase other properties as investors. It was my turn to take a swing at life, and it was a direct hit. Pat Murphy was on his way! We managed to acquire properties in several states, but our primary holdings were in Texas. I'll tell you more about that later.

Now that our wealth was growing, we were finally able to move out of that Habitat for Humanity home. We built a lovely home in Patterson, California. What a home it was. It was 3,600 immaculate square feet. The dream of a larger home had finally come true. God had kissed our cheeks again and we kissed his right back.

We lived in our Patterson home for several years until, one day, my next door neighbor told us about a new home he was having built in Texas. He came over to our house one afternoon to show us his blueprints. My home was nice, but nothing in comparison to what he showed us. The kicker was how much he was paying for his new castle. When I saw the price, I was instantly blown away. The home was twice the size of ours at half the price. It was a no-brainer. We had a family meeting about relocating, and that was that. Texas, here we come.

We began flying back and forth between California and Texas to work with the builders on our new miniature mansion. At least, I thought it was a miniature mansion. It was an expansive 7,000 square feet; we were moving up. As a gift to myself, we moved to Texas permanently on my birthday. By then, our net worth had reached close to $2 million dollars. We had finally made it to the big leagues.

Shortly after moving to Texas, we found a church we liked called The Potter's House. I found the preacher to be very insightful. His deep, booming voice wouldn't allow anyone to fall asleep during his sermons. About a year later, I joined their children's ministry. I became a youth leader. Every Sunday, I would have an average of 150 to 200 students in my class. I later found out that the daughter of a famous football player by the name of Emmitt Smith attended my class weekly. I was finally enjoying the lifestyle I had dreamed about all those years ago, until...

Our wonderful dream life lasted for almost a decade. But in 2007, it came crashing down around us. Many of you will remember the real estate and stock market crash in 2008 and 2009. However, I started seeing signs of a change in 2006 and 2007. I noticed it, but didn't know what to do about it. I learned then that it is entirely possible to have enough information to reach the summit of your dreams and still lack the knowledge required to remain there. We spent ten years painstakingly building our net worth only to have it whittled away in two years. We were back at square one, only this time we had no money and bad credit as well. Our credit scores had been decimated due to the foreclosures of some of our investment properties. I knew how to buy properties, but I had failed to educate myself on how to put them in a business name or an

LLC. Every aspect of our business was in our personal names. It was a costly mistake.

It wasn't long before the pressure of money took its toll on my family. As the bills piled up, so did the stress. A few years later, our marriage of 27 years evaporated. The divorce was finalized. The friends I had were gone. Pat Murphy was gone. I had not only lost my marriage and friends, but I had lost myself. Not all of me, but rather a huge part of who I was. A part of me was gone; a part of me was still hanging around, but which parts were which? How can you move on when you don't know who you're moving on with? Which part of me was supposed to move on? And move on to where? This was the beginning of the funeral service for Pat Murphy, and it was a confusing beginning.

One day, in the midst of my breakdown, I spoke to a young man. I asked him how he felt about himself and about his feelings on the subject of self-love. His response was tragic. He told me that the idea of self-love was something he had been struggling with for the last few years. He explained, "I ask myself, 'What is there to love about me?' And I can never come up with an answer." At hearing his story, I thought to myself, "This young man must be lost," and I knew it was true, for that young man was me. In that moment of self-reflection, I knew I had lost all direction.

During the following years, I battled with the issues of self-value and self-love. I had become blind to my value and what I had to offer myself and the world. An exploration of my heart told me that the reason I was playing host to these issues was simply that I placed value on myself based on the mistakes I made in life. The accumulation of my mistakes and losses caused me to no longer see anything worthwhile about me. Looking in the mirror was such a challenge. I remember during that time I would never look myself in the eyes while brushing my hair because the face and eyes that looked back at me were reflecting nothing but a failure; a failure to my family, a failure to my God, and most of all, a failure to myself. What was there to be proud of? What was there to celebrate? The only answer I had was, "nothing.".

What a terrible outlook on life. I tried pursuing good deeds. I tried to continue to do nice things for people. I tried to be polite. I tried to smile all the time in hopes it would fix my depressed state of mind, but it did not. Even those attempts failed. Going to church and praying didn't seem to help either. Although the Bible says that God loves us no matter what, when your heart is fractured, it is hard for you to tell what love is. It could smack you in the face, but you would be too drowsy from sorrow to notice what was being offered to you.

Psychologically, failure did something to me deep on the inside. Fear and doubt became my best friends. Having tried and tried, failure after failure, I began to believe that success may be for some, but not for me. How can one believe in themselves when failure seems to be their constant companion?

I don't know when it happened, but eventually I came to realize something. There was going to be a war in my mind. A war had to be waged to reclaim the throne of life from the self-loathing that had claimed it. The alternative was to continue to allow my life to leak away. My drive, my resolution, and my passion were seeping from my being, and I feared that, ultimately, I would consider death a sweet resolve.

The Pain of Cracks in Your Life

ave you ever seen a vase or decorative jar that is suffering from "stress fractures" try to hold water? At the Potter's House, there use to be large pictures on either side of the stage, one hanging on the right and another on the left. Each picture depicted a tall clay jar filled with water. The jars were tilted slightly to allow the water inside them to spill to the ground. However, each of the jars also had small cracks running down their sides. Water was shown escaping from these cracks, streaming to the ground to join that which poured from the top. During services, I would look at those images and be brought to tears. They were the perfect metaphor for my life at that time. The more I tried, the more I cracked. Soon enough, my cracked soul was leaking everywhere. I've never felt pain like those delivered by those cracks. I seemed to spend more time crying during services than listening to the sermon or singing along with the choir. I was losing myself. Drip by drip. Drop after drop. It's hard to survive when you have more leaking out of you than you have coming in. I felt drained and empty. I used to have a backup water supply; it has a bright and shiny label that read "Pat Murphy." But, I had misplaced myself somewhere. "Where did I put myself? Has anyone seen where I put Pat Murphy?" I would lament, but no one heard my grief. The only person I ever asked was myself, and I never seemed to answer.

When you keep asking for answers and can find none, many of us seek resolution from the one place that should have all the answers. Sadly, that place often appears silent when we need noise to fill our souls the most. In our search, we turn to God. I know I did. I asked Him for answers. I asked Him for guidance, but he replied with silence. I repeated my questions with anger, shouting into the stillness, but God did not seem to hear me.

Since God didn't seem to want to help me, I thought I might as well stop helping Him. I no longer taught in the children's ministry. For a while, I still continued to try to help people inside and outside the church, but I was doing it from an empty place. Finally, I gave that up as well. I no longer wanted to serve anything or anyone. My jar was empty. My heart was empty. I had nothing left to give. Have you ever tried to serve others from an empty water pot? Are you currently trying to give from an empty heart?

Eventually, anger flooded my empty vessel. I was full again, but full of anger towards God. Yes, I wanted to indict God for allowing me such suffering and loss. I railed against him. I continued to ask questions, but they were more like accusations. I would shout, "How could You allow such pain in my life?" "For years, I told people about Your grace and Your mercy, but now that I need some of that goodness for myself You are silent." I would shout and cry while never receiving a response. "No problem," I decided. "If You're silent, I can be silent, as well."

So, I began to come home from work and enclose myself in my room. Shutting the door to my bedroom was like shutting the door to the world and everyone in it, God included. For three months, my life consisted of nothing more than me and that room. My bedroom became a prison cell of my own making. I saved myself from the efforts of interacting physically or emotionally with anyone, but at the cost of locking my heart away from love. I no longer saw my efforts in life as necessary. Writing this now, I guess that's where I lost myself. After all this time, I know where I left Pat Murphy. I left him in that room. I walked out of that room and went to work. I even went to church, though I'm not sure why I continued to go. However, it wasn't really me. It was my shadow. The shadow of the man that once existed. The real Pat Murphy lay in the tomb known as "my bed." I needed a resurrection. I knew there was only one person who could pull it off; He'd done it once before for Lazarus. But I had stopped trusting the Giver of Life some time ago. What were the odds that He would help me now? Besides, had He rescued me in the first place, I would never have lost myself, right? After all that had transpired, I figured that asking Him to bring me back to life would be a waste of time. He was probably too busy running the world to care about little, insignificant me, anyway. Maybe that's why He allowed me to die to begin with. When I had asked for help, He was busy answering other people's prayers, and He did not have time for me. I mean, who was I anyway? I was not a famous actor or a preacher. I was not a well-known motivational speaker or a world leader. I was sure that if I had been someone like that, He would have instantly given me what I wanted. But me? I was nothing more than a Pat Murphy. As the old timers used to say, "britches and breath." Each day seemed the same. People would say to me, "thank God for another day to be alive." I never said out loud the words that were in my mind. Still, I thought, "Thank him for another day? For what? Another day like yesterday or like last week or last month? To hell with today. If it wasn't for my children, what reason would there have been to keep going on in this wretched place called earth?" There was one thing that I had forgotten to take into account, however. I had forgotten that old adage, "God works in mysterious ways." He's working, even when we don't realize it, and he brought someone back into my life that would hold my hand and help me look for the part of me I had lost.

It seemed like chance that I reconnected with my old friend. She was kind and gentle in her attempts to understand what had happened to her old buddy Pat. After she got off work, she would come home, make a cup of green tea, and allow this broken man to sit with her on her patio and talk. She would sip her tea and listen intently as I opened the door to my heart. She helped me to remove one brick at a time from the wall I had erected within myself. She was patient. She never condemned me or anyone to whom I claimed to have issues with, including God. It was as though I was speaking with my own private angel. At the end of each green tea meeting, I found myself looking forward to the next. Interacting with her wasn't the exhausting sort of labor I had assumed opening up would be. Each meeting allowed the wall inside of me to fall, until one day, I went home to my tomb and finally slept in peace.

The next morning, for the first time in quite a while, I drew the curtains and allowed the sunshine to pour into my burial chamber. I didn't understand it. I found myself asking, "What's going on here? Who's this rising from my bed in the morning?" Over time, I even mustered the courage to brush my hair while looking myself in the eye, and I didn't want to vomit. I was back! Or was I? Something was definitely different, but it had been so long since I had seen the old Pat, that I couldn't be sure if this was him. I saw me, but it was not the me I remembered from the past, and it was not the me with the hurt and pain, either. I recognized the facial features of this Pat, but not the eyes. There seemed to be a small ember of light in this Pat's eyes. That light cast a happy glow that suggested that he was glad to be alive today. "Where did you come from?" I asked my reflection. "Who the hell are you, and what did you do with the other Pat Murphy?"

The new Pat refused to vacate the premises. It was

an invasion of the body snatchers. But I came to like him. He not only arose from the bed with a little pep in his step, but he dressed differently, too. He actually cared about what he was going to put on for that day and the impression it would make. He ensured that every strand of the remaining hairs of his head looked orderly. He smiled when looking in the mirror. "Wow!" I thought. "I must admit that I kinda like this guy." This was a Pat Murphy I had not seen in years, and he became pretty cool to hang around. I noticed that his energy level really went into overdrive when it was time to go see his buddy, the green tea lady.

During their last few discussions, he no longer whined about the people who hurt him or betrayed him. No, he spoke of the sunlight that brightened the day and the blue skies that seemed to listen in on their conversations. He could hear the birds chirping in the trees, and he felt the wind that blew across his brow. Yes. He was feeling again. He was alive again. Did the Giver of Life resurrect Pat Murphy? But how did He do it? He didn't say anything to me like he did to Lazarus. There was no, "Come forth." No angels were standing outside my tomb announcing to the world that I had risen from the dead like they did for Jesus. I wasn't sure how it had happened, but I concluded that it could be nothing short of a miracle.

Being angry with God hinders the heart's ear from hearing the sweet and soft voice of our Creator. He does not shout. He whispers into our soul. Oftentimes, we cannot hear His voice; our internal noise makers, stress, anxiety and fear, are far too loud. Therefore, he must move on to plan B, speaking through others. The green tea lady, Nancy, was the voice God used to speak to me. He had never left or abandoned me at all. I just couldn't hear Him through the pain. My own self-condemnation, brought on by my failures, clouded my judgement and dulled my ability to hear His voice.

God, I never told You sorry for treating you the way I did. I want to thank You for not giving up on me when I turned my back on You and gave up on myself. Thank You for sending Your angel, "the green tea lady," to tell this Lazarus to come forth out of his self-inflicted tomb, and to arise from the nightmare of my own making. Many of you reading this book, may still be living in a nightmare of your own creation.

Today, I write from the mind of the new Pat Murphy. Everything is not completely rosy, but I discovered that how I choose to see my problems and failures will either bury me or elevate me. The choice is mine. Preparing for possible problems, rather than being a victim to them, permits me to take a proactive approach in the outcome of my life. I start by prayer and meditation with God. Prayer is me talking. Meditation is sitting quietly and letting God talk to me. It's a two-way conversation. I now realize one of my mistakes, which so many people make as well, was talking too much and not listening enough. We pray, but do not meditate. He hears us, but we don't give Him a chance to respond. How could I be angry with God when I wasn't even listening? I began to read my bible more diligently. Not reading just to say "I read today," but to seek answers. I also read books from authors who conquered life's challenges and have come back to tell of their stories of triumph. I equipped my mind to be able to handle any challenge without falling under the weight of it. Also, Pat Murphy married his green tea angel, and they are doing wonderful works around the world. When an angel comes into your life, do not let them fly away.

There are 17 golden nuggets of wisdom that I learned through my experiences that I would like to share with you, the reader. Hopefully they will bless you as they did me.

Golden Nugget #1
Surviving Your Thoughts

*W*hat you believe in your heart about yourself will always be true in your mind. How you process information, make decisions, and go about your day all stem from your belief of self. This is a tough lesson to learn when you are going through life's challenges. It is very difficult to recognize that your own thoughts can become your enemy, but making an enemy of your thoughts is easy. You start with the appearance that life is winning the boxing match against you, and that you are powerless to do anything about it. Then, you add to that the fact that life's little minions, which we call people, will say some of the nastiest things to and about you to make you believe that you are not a gift from God. Finally, you mix in a string of failed attempts at your goals, and there you have it, a living person with a lifeless mind.

In order to restore the spark of life to your thoughts, you have to reevaluate your thought process. You must storm the castle walls and reclaim the throne of your mind. The overlord of lies and deceptions has taken control of your mental kingdom and made all your decisions subject to his dark biddings. Motivational pep talks and prayers are helpful, but in the end, you must do the work. For many, this fight will literally mean life or death. Many who will become victims of suicide believe that they have nothing to live for. In other words, they think, "I have no value, so why remain alive?" This train of thought reminds me of one of my mentor's, Og Mandino. He did a talk one time to an audience explaining how he came to be one of the world's most influential writers. I believe his book *The Greatest Salesman in the World* is still the number one bestselling book for sales professionals, even though it was written a few decades ago. I listened to his video on YouTube the other day, and I was surprised to find out that he admitted to wanting to end his life prior to writing that book and his many others. Had he followed his depressed thoughts and purchased the gun he was contemplating using, millions of lives would not have been changed by his writings. That includes mine. He has since passed away, but as Dr. Myles Monroe, one of my other mentors said, "Die empty." We will all go to the grave one day, but let's not hasten the process. You and I have much to offer this world and many hidden gifts and talents inside of us. Let's go on a treasure hunt to see what is buried on the inside of us and display that for the world to admire.

Golden Nugget #2

The Importance of Self Love and Self Esteem

Self-love simply means to love one's self. The word self-esteem means to know your estimated value. It is important to know that your life has value and that you are not an accident. You were created with a purpose. If you have endured family failures, relationship failures, business failures, etc. time and again, an erosion begins to take place in your mind and heart. Erosion of the soul also occurs when one believes the negative words of others. The mental acceptance of their information causes many to see themselves not for who they truly are and what gifts they possess, but rather, by the way others see them, no matter how wrong they may be. Your belief in their words will have you valuing yourself at the price of a penny when you are a priceless treasure. In order to elaborate on this point, I would like to tell you a short story.

THE LITTLE BOY AND THE SHINING ROCKS

There used to be a road, long, old, and dusty, that was of no use to anyone anymore, save a small boy who liked to walk along its overgrown ditches, picking up rocks. He'd select a stone, weigh it in his hand, rear back, and hurl it as far as his scrawny arms could muster. The little boy would spend his day seeing how far he could toss the rocks, gathering dust stains as he went. His family was very poor. His mother and father worked hard to provide for him, but that meant that he was often alone. His favorite things in the world were that road and those rocks.

One day, he happened upon a cave in the cliff face that lined one side of his road. The little sunlight that penetrated the darkness of the cavern illuminated the shiniest rocks the boy had ever seen. He filled his pockets with the shining stones and continued his walk, tossing the glistening pebbles as he went. Each day, the boy would go back to the cave, fill his pockets with shining stones, and throw them this way and that along the abandoned road.

Not long after the discovery of the cave, the boy's father chanced to have a day off work. Together, the two kicked at the dust along the old, forgotten road, the son delighted to have his father with him in his favorite place, the father was overjoyed to be sharing his son's favorite pass time. The boy headed straight for the cave, excited to show his dad the place where the shining stones were hidden. When they arrived, the the boy began to gather the stones as usual, filling his pockets with enough stones to throw.

Meanwhile, his father examined the veins of stones that ran through the walls of the cave. Their golden yellow was reflective even in the sparse sunlight.

"Eureka!" exclaimed the father, his jubilation echoing off the cavern walls. The son, startled by his father's enthusiasm, asked what eureka meant. To which his father replied, "I've made a discovery. Your shining stones are more than stones, my boy. They're gold!" What had been little more than a child's play thing went on to make the boy and his family the wealthiest family in history.

The point of that story was to illustrate the fact that we have gold on the inside of us, but, unless we dig deeper within ourselves, we may only see plain old rocks. You have more worth than you realize, just like that little boy's shining stones.

Could this be you right now? Are you seeing plain rocks when you are truly a priceless treasure? Are you looking in the mirror with disdain for the one looking back at you? Do you love and accept yourself regardless of where you are in life today? If you truly knew how wonderful you are, would it make a difference in how you treat your body? Would you smile again? Self-love and self-esteem are the twins of a healthy emotional person. They provide balance and equilibrium when your world seems unstable and out of control. They will remind you of who you truly are regardless of your mistakes or failures. They will center your mind when all else may be off kilter. Lastly, self-love and self-esteem are found within, not without. People and circumstances may change, but your worth will not. Because your worth is not depended on who sees your value or who chooses to throw you away like the little boy who didn't realize what he had in his possession. I think you get the point for now, but we'll discuss self-love in relationships a bit later.

Golden Nugget #3

Your Circumstances Do Not Determine Your

Value

It took time, but I had to learn and accept that circumstances will change. However, my outlook on life and the way I see myself do not necessarily have to change with them. Circumstances are like the wind. They blow in and out of our lives. Indicting yourself for not handling a circumstance that you probably weren't trained to handle, serves little purpose. Self-pity and self-defeating thoughts are the key to your destruction. The one thing that everyone forgets is that change will happen to us all, no matter what.

I was praying one time, and the Lord gave me

something to anchor my thoughts to whenever I feel lost. He said "You cannot control the flow of the river, so just learn to paddle through the waves." I have this statement on my vision board. Are you disappointed with yourself because you feel as though you should've been in control of the situation? Maybe you could have been and maybe you couldn't. Either way, beating yourself up over it will not help you. Change of thought and the wisdom of the lesson learned can equip you to not repeat the same mistake again. I sent out a quote today to my friends on Groupme. It said, *"There is a big difference between what we wanted to happen and what is actually happening. Come to that truth and freedom of the mind eagerly awaits you."*

Golden Nugget #4

You Cannot Win with a Mind Full of Doubt

You can never win in business or anything else, until the battle has been won in your mind. Now this is not to say that you will not be afraid. As Susan Jeffers's book title says, "Feel the Fear and Do It Anyway." Fear and other emotions are natural. However, to make an attempt at anything, you must believe in yourself. You must believe that you can accomplish that which you set out to do. If you do not believe that you can accomplish it, then why try in the first place? One of the best ways to overcome doubt and fear is by knowledge. Knowledge can be considered synonymous with information. Could it be that you're suffering a lot of failures, as I did, because you simply did not have enough information? I tried so many business ventures simply because of the sales pitches and the promises of great success. There were promises of riches and wealth, but I did not have enough information to perform the tasks at hand. I saw many successful people in the same business, but success always seemed to elude me. I now understand why I failed so often. I did not educate myself enough on what it would take to succeed in that arena before attempting my pursuit. This in fact was the root of my failure in many business ventures. Had I invested in my mind, I probably would have suffered fewer failures. I suffered doubt because of my lack of knowledge. The more knowledge you have of any subject or endeavor the less intimidating it will be. The less intimidating the situation, the more confident you are of the outcome. The more confident you are the higher the chance of success.

I also learned that many of us try to do too many things at once instead of focusing on one task at a time. We're like that old saying, "Jack of all trades master of none." Could it be possible that you are suffering defeat and failure because you are attempting to do too many things at the same time? Or could it be possible that you were never meant to do some of the things you are trying to accomplish in the first place? That sure was true in my life. That is why I could not win in my mind; I was focused on the wrong things. Some of the things I pursued, I was never created to do; therefore, failure was inevitable. I caused my own downfall by chasing the wind. *An unfocused mind will constantly suffer defeat and failure.*

Golden Nugget #5

The Importance of Self-Love in Relationships

Self-love is a very important subject. However, it seems to find itself last on the list when it comes to the discussion of relational love. How can you know and identify what love is or what love looks like if you do not have it for yourself? That is why, oftentimes, we seek relationships with other people to help us feel better about ourselves. There is a scripture in the Bible where Jesus is asked what the greatest commandment is. His answer was eye opening. In Matthew 22:36-40 (NIV), it says, "Teacher, which is the greatest commandment in the Law?" Jesus replied, "Love the Lord your God with all your heart and with all your soul and with all your mind.' This is the first and greatest commandment. And the second is like it: 'Love your neighbor as yourself.' All the Law and the Prophets hang on these two commandments." The odd part of his answer is the fact that he said to love your neighbor "**as yourself.**" It's amazing to me how many people are looking for love. It is very risky to look for love from other people without having it for yourself first.

There is a great tragedy happening in our country today. This tragedy contributes to our divorce rates being at an all-time high. What is this great tragedy? It is people who are looking for love in all the wrong places like Johnny Lee's old song talked about. People think that they will find love at a club, at church, or at the workplace. There are even numerous dating sites claiming to help you find love. These are not all the wrong places, necessarily, but they certainly can be. Why? Because love must begin in your own heart. You must start the search for love within yourself. This is what we call self-love. Self-love is not egotistical or self-ish. In fact, it is the very opposite. When you have self-love, you are equipped to give love instead of being in a desperate search for love from others. When two people with self-love come together, you now have a loving couple that can go the relational distance. Most people see a relationship from a 50/50 point of you. If you do the math, 50% + 50% = 100%. You may think that is a healthy relationship according to those numbers. But wait, what if someone in the relationship is only giving 30% while the other is giving 50%, now you only have 80%. Let's try 60% + 40% = 100%. Now we are back at 100. Wonderful. But, according to that equation, in order to have 100%, someone is giving more than the other. Keeping the relationship at that level, the possibility of someone feeling slighted or used most often come into play which creates tension and resentment. So, let's do the math from a self-love perspective. If I love myself 100% and I meet someone who loves themselves 100%, now we are in a position to give love from a reservoir of completeness rather than one in need of being filled. $100\% + 100\% = 200\%$. So, from the beginning, our odds are better off than the 50/50 position. Let's say that one day I'm not feeling my emotional best and my number goes down to 80% and my wife is still at 100%. We are still operating at a 180% success rate. Much better numbers than the 50/50. Let's say we are both at 75%. Our combined love number will be 150%. As you can see, even on a bad day, we still have plenty of love to share because we started from a position of completeness and not a depleted state of being. This point is crucial and will help you in our next topic.

Do you love yourself? Honestly, do you? The Bible says that in order for you to love your neighbor, your wife, your husband, your children, your friends, and even strangers, you must love yourself first. Therefore, if you do not love yourself, how can you possibly love someone else? And if you do not love yourself, how is it possible for you to identify what real love is from anyone else? If God is love, then how can you recognize Him if you do not know what love is? How can you recognize when He is trying to express love to you if you are not familiar with love? As you can see, if you do not have self-love, it is hard for you to detect love anywhere else.

Could you possibly be suffering failure in relationships because of your lack of self-love? I agree with the idea of finding love in all the wrong places, because so many people are seeking love outside of themselves and not inside of their own hearts. So, if you want to know the great secret to having long-lasting and loving relationships, it is to love yourself. One should be able to share love from an internal, abundant storehouse. In other words, because you love yourself so much, you have plenty left over to share and to give to other people. Consequently, you are no longer seeking love from other people all the time, but rather giving love from your abundance.

Through hardship, I have learned to love and appreciate myself. I examine how I feel about myself quite often to ensure that I never again fall into the trap of self-hatred. I now give love to those in need of it, because I have more than enough for myself. I still make blunders from time to time, but I do not devalue myself because of them. Moreover, I now understand that regardless of who comes and goes, what goes right or wrong, Pat Murphy is still a person worth loving, even if I must be the only one to do it. If you really absorb what I am sharing in this chapter, you will begin to understand why the people you thought should have loved you could not. They may have been depleted of self-love and could not love you the way you thought they should. This will help you forgive people that disappointed you. It will help you to love rather than hate people for their shortcomings.

Golden Nugget #6
Do not Fall Apart Because They Left

I read somewhere, *"Some people are going to leave, but that's not the end of your story. That's the end of their part in your story…"* Attempting to hang on to people who want to leave is very damaging to your emotional stability. There is a great book by Steve Grissom and Kathy Leonard called, *Divorce Care*. In the book, they share how a person who is going through a breakup or divorce divides their emotional energy. Grissom and Leonard say that, when going through a split, 85 percent of a person's emotional energy goes toward trying to stabilize how they feel about the situation, while only 15 percent is left to handle work, children, and other challenges in their lives. Could it be possible that you are currently suffering from emotional imbalance? Could it be that your emotional equilibrium is not centered? This certainly was the case for me at that time. I couldn't tell up from down or heads from tails. My emotions followed the lead of a confused mind, and since my mind was a mess so were my emotions.

You are not a failure because a person wanted to leave. This holds true in business as well as in relationships. Too often, we define ourselves by who stays and who leaves. The mistake is to think that if anybody leaves us, there must be something wrong with us. Let me pass something on to you that was told to me a while back that really helped: **everyone has agendas.** Do not forget this fact. Everyone, including you, has an agenda. Some people have good agendas, while others' are not so good. Some people come into our lives with conditions. Some of these conditions or expectations may include money, sex, companionship, etc. These conditions are predicated upon the fact that if we fulfill their wish list, they may stay, but if we ever stop checking off that list, they may simply leave. All you can do is your best. If that is not good enough for them, then oh well; let them leave. If you are looking to people to fulfill your agenda, then you are the person in error. This is neither fair to the other person nor to yourself. Quite often, our agendas stem from the need for love as we discussed earlier. When it comes to love, love freely from your abundance, not from a deficit. This will help you to not be a user of people.

Another piece of advice I heard from Dr. Myles Monroe, was to never assume everyone loves you for you. Many people claim to love you for the fruit that you bear, meaning, the gifts, talents or anything else they are the beneficiaries of. Let me give you an example. If I was offering to give a thousand people one million dollars each, people all over the world would suddenly contact me non stop. Are they doing so because they love me? Of course not. They are doing so because of what I have to offer. Therefore, it would be foolish of me to think that all those people are contacting me because they love me. They are simply seeking the fruit that I bear. As long as I have this rectified in my mind, I will be fine, but if I lose sight of this principle, I invite pain into my life. Very few people will be in your life just for you and nothing more. Unconditional love is hard to find. If you be so lucky as I when I found it with my green tea angel, keep them in your life. These people are rare individuals indeed.

Golden Nugget #7

Failure Is Not Your Identity

Calling yourself a failure and having failed at something are two different things. I've done both. Too many times, people adopt the idea that if they've failed at something that makes them a failure. That was my thought process for quite some time. The difference between the two concepts depends on how you view them. **Are you breastfeeding your failed attempts as though they were your babies, or did you simply fail at something**? To be a failure is to admit that nothing you try will ever succeed, and that can only happen if you quit. To have failed at something means that a mistake was possibly made or that you may need more knowledge to achieve what you are trying to pursue. So, it is vitally important that you never accept circumstances as the defining factor of who you are. This was a fatal mistake that I made for many years. When I failed at something, I considered myself a failure. I realize now that if I keep on trying and don't give up, that alone makes me a success and not a failure.

Some people walk around wearing their failure like a badge of honor, collecting self-pity along the pathway of their lives. What could they possibly hope to gain by constantly putting themselves down? If you keep putting yourself down, you can never pull yourself back up. **There is no profit in pity, especially self-pity.** Neither should there be shame in your failed attempts to succeed. To have failed means you've tried; that alone is something that you should be proud of. Looking back on my failed attempts to succeed has given me a new perspective of myself. I now see that even when I was afraid, I tried. When others said I couldn't do it, I still tried. When I didn't have enough money, I tried. When others resolved to live normal lives, I attempted to be great. I did not give up. I am still trying, which means I still haven't given up. My dark years were nothing more than a pause in my efforts to succeed. Life was testing my persistence. And although I have not achieved the success I seek as of yet, I now have the strength of mind to not give up on myself for having tried. These are not the character-istics of a failure.

How could I possibly have considered myself a failure? A failure does not get up and continue striving towards success. A failure will lie down and quit. I did not lie down and quit. Notice the word "lie." It was all a mental lie. I got back up from the mat time and time again after getting beat down in the boxing match of life. I got back up. I got knocked down. I got back up again. I never quit. I kept going. And although I still have not achieved the massive success that I dreamed about, I am still breathing, therefore, I still have an opportunity. The dream that was always alive in my heart is still there. I believe the same holds true for you. This is the power of our wills when they are connected to our minds. We have the ability to will ourselves back into the fight and to push ourselves to success when we feel like giving up.

If you have tried and your attempts have not worked out the way you thought they should, it's okay. At least you tried. There are two things you can do from here. You can try again at the same goal and continue as often as needed until you succeed, or you can pursue another goal. Do not waste your life wallowing in self-pity over the things you did not accomplish. Time is the one commodity that no one can afford to waste, so use it wisely. Go back to the drawing board. Reinvest in your mind by getting the knowledge necessary to accomplish your goals, then try again. Trying does not make you a failure, it makes you courageous. When I fail, my self-love keeps me going. I now understand that every failed attempt does not require me to give up on myself. I tell others what I have told myself numerous times, D.G.U., D.G.U., D.G.U. It stands for DON'T GIVE UP. There is a book that helped me along my journey. It's a book by John C. Maxwell called *Failing Forward. Turning Mistakes into Stepping Stones for Success*. I highly recommend getting this book and incorporating his concepts into your mind today. Keep forging ahead.

Golden Nugget #8

Mentor Your Way to the Top

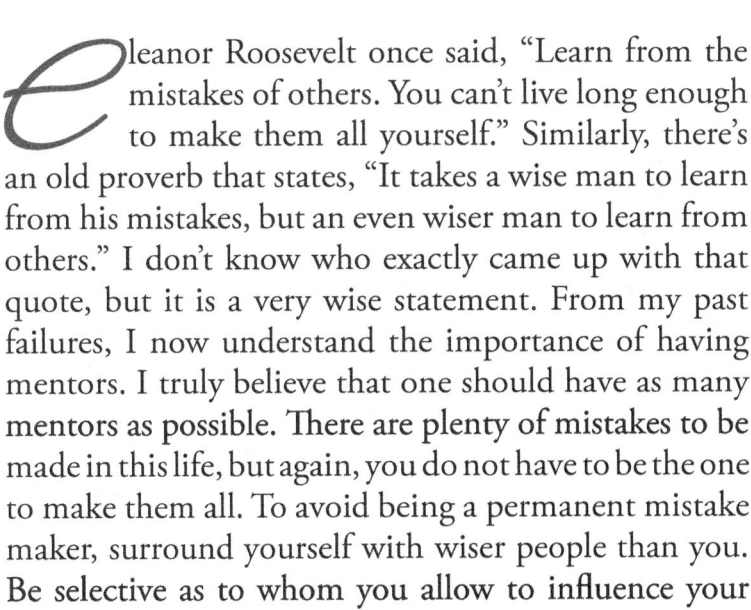

leanor Roosevelt once said, "Learn from the mistakes of others. You can't live long enough to make them all yourself." Similarly, there's an old proverb that states, "It takes a wise man to learn from his mistakes, but an even wiser man to learn from others." I don't know who exactly came up with that quote, but it is a very wise statement. From my past failures, I now understand the importance of having mentors. I truly believe that one should have as many mentors as possible. There are plenty of mistakes to be made in this life, but again, you do not have to be the one to make them all. To avoid being a permanent mistake maker, surround yourself with wiser people than you. Be selective as to whom you allow to influence your life, for what you hear, your mind will receive, and what your mind receives, it will believe. Many of you who are reading this book consider yourself a failure because of the words of other people. Therefore, it is important for you to be very cautious who you allow to speak into your life. **Negative words equal negative thoughts. Positive words equal positive thoughts.**

Mentors can play a vital role in to your success. It is very wise to seek out mentors in the field where you are attempting to find success. If they have succeeded already in what you are attempting to do, why not ask for their advice? Common mistakes can be avoided by simply asking for advice from those who are front-runners in your marketplace. Now, I can hear you say, "What if I do not know of any such mentors?" I use to ask the same question, until I discovered the value of books and YouTube. Some of my mentors, such as Dr. Myles Munroe and Og Mandino, are individuals who have passed away some time ago. However, their books and videos are still mentoring my mind to this very day. I also watch people that I admire that are unaware that they are mentoring me. People such as my old friend Mark Nusbaum, Bishop T.D Jakes, Iyanla Vanzant, Oprah Winfrey, Dr. Conway Edwards at One Community Church, Steve Harvey, Tai Lopez, and many others. I watch their mannerisms. I watch how they handle stressful situations. I watch how they speak and how they make business decisions. They are mentoring me on how to conduct myself now and when I get to their level. My mentors' achievements and their ability to never quit has been priceless to me.

They provide a lush garden of fruits and vegetables to nourish my mind when I am hungry for encouragement. Never minimize the power of mentorship. This mistake is common among those who consider themselves failures. But if you ever listen to successful people or read their books, you will see that they also made many mistakes. They just did not consider themselves a failure. They learned that in order to succeed you will make mistakes. These lessons were taught to them by their mentors. Many of the most successful people in the world have mentors. We all need mentors. That is one of the keys to success.

Another issue that causes many to fail is the belief that we cannot trust other people, and therefore, must do everything alone. Upon deeper reflection, this comes from negative thought patterns and possibly having the wrong people in your life. Look at who's around you. Who are your closest friends? Are they attempting to achieve anything significant like you are? What family members do you feed and glean information from? Are you gaining counsel from wise people, or are you simply trying to figure it all out by yourself? These mistakes are common among those who consider themselves failures. I consistently made these same mistakes, but as I said, even the greats made mistakes. Thomas A. Edison, the inventor of the light bulb, said, "I have not failed. I've just found 10,000 ways that won't work."

Golden Nugget #9

Yesterday Is Over

*T*here is a grave danger in keeping your thoughts focused on yesterdays. Yesterdays always seem to carry the memory of what we did not accomplish. They remember failed relationships, failed attempts at business, disappointments, and sorrows. Unfortunately, we hardly ever remember the good that happened in our yesterdays. For some reason, the mind is geared towards focusing primarily on bad experiences with a few sprinkles of good ones on top. What purpose do my yesterdays serve? If yesterday is not serving as my teacher, then why do I need its echoes in my mind? Why allow my mind to revisit my yesterdays over and over only to torment me with memories of failed attempts?

I think we humans have a glitch in our heads that causes us to focus primarily on that which is negative, especially when reminiscing. If our minds remain trapped in the challenges of yesterday, it will derail any attempts at success today. And if today is stripped of use and energy because of our focus on yesterday, then tomorrow's success will inevitably result in failure. It is a vicious cycle, but one of our own creation. This was my experience, until I realized that today is all I have. If we spend our today on yesterday, then our tomorrow is doomed. I read a book by Eckhart Tolle called, *The Power of Now*. This book helped clear the cobwebs from my mind. I then understood why God told Moses in Exodus 3:14 "I Am that I Am…" He did not say "I was," or, "I will be." He said, "I Am." I Am, being present tense. Therefore, I shall live in the present tense where God dwells.

Before coming to this realization, I was treading water. I kept asking, "Why didn't things work out?" when I should have been asking "What's next?" I have discovered a small secret to avoiding depression. **Stop asking the why!** Asking why things turned out the way they did kept my mind tied to negative events. I kept trying to rationalize and find answers to questions that had no relevance to my present or my future. When I started asking "What's next?" my mind begin to move forward. I now remind myself everyday to live like time; time doesn't stop and neither should I. Time moves forward regardless of what the day brings. It doesn't pause to figure out why the sun cast its warmth upon the earth, or why the moon cast its glow. It doesn't inquire as to why God does what He does, and it doesn't consult with me as to whether my attempts at success failed or not. It has one goal in mind. Keep going. Don't stop. We must learn from our mentor, time. Keep going, and never stop. Never quit, and never give up.

Golden Nugget #10

Yesterday Thoughts Smothers Today's

Opportunities

There is something else that poses a problem when it comes to yesterdays. Negative memories of yesterdays restrain our creative mind. They hinder your ability to create fresh ideas for what we can accomplish today. For example, if I spend today depressed over my failed attempts at business from yesterday, how much energy do I really have to think of ways to succeed tomorrow? As the old saying goes, turn lemons into lemonade. But how can one accomplish building a lemonade stand if they are always upset about the apple juice stand that failed yesterday? When was the last time you turned a lemon into lemonade? Are you still hanging onto the lemon wishing it would turn into apple juice?

I was reading a book by Og Mandino called *The Greatest Salesman in The World Part II*, and it said something very insightful that I thought I would share with you. It talked about how some people sit around waiting for opportunities, while others create opportunities for themselves. Oftentimes, we do not create opportunities for ourselves because we develop an "I've done that before, and it did not work out, so why try again," attitude. So, we simply just give up on ourselves. Then we turn right back around and start being upset with the way our life is turning out. You can only win a race when you run the race. Even if you fall down on the track, to complete the race, you still must get up and run again. If you're sitting on the track constantly crying about having fell, you forfeit the race. The fact that you're lying on the track and not attempting to get up again makes you a failure, not the fall. I define failure as simply giving up. You must get into your mind the idea of, "Yes I have fallen, but what do I need to do next to complete the task?" Don't be like that elderly lady in the famous commercial who said, "I've fallen, and I can't get up." You can get up as many times as necessary. Keep getting up until you win. This will shift your mind from self-pity to successful thinking. And even if you must limp to the finish line, at least you were able to make it there where your lemonade stand awaits. Be proud of the fact that you did not allow yesterday's failures to prevent you from reaching for today's opportunities.

Golden Nugget #11
How Our Yesterdays Create Depression

ocusing on yesterdays presents another hazard, as well. By constantly wondering what happened, you are inviting depression into your life. One of the big mistakes I made after my divorce and business failures was continually asking the questions why and what? Why did it happen? What did I do wrong? What could I have done better? Why didn't my marriage work out? I asked myself a million questions. I asked them over and over and over again, but I always ended up with the same result, depression. Depression had become my new companion. I dated depression. I married depression. It was my new bedfellow. But, when I learned to stop asking those questions, I divorced depression. Depression and I are no longer on speaking terms. When depression comes calling, I hang up the phone. I blocked depression's number. I have a restraining order out on depression. It tries to find me, but I'm in a witness protection program, so it will always fail. We do not get along, depression and I, and neither should depression and you get along.

My definition of depression is simply "deep pressure." It is pressure deep in the heart which deters your forward progress. It is your responsibility as well as mine to make sure that we do not allow our minds to remain in the yesterdays of failure. Failure obstructs our thinking and so does depression. They serve no purpose. To divorce depression, you must divorce the repetitive, negative thoughts that attack your mind. If other people's negative words have been spoken into your life in your yesterdays, divorce those words as well. That was their idea of you, which is not the truth of you. All thoughts that hinder your thinking should no longer be accepted. Hit the delete button in your mind as often as necessary, and think your way free. The choice is yours just like it was mine.

Golden Nugget #12

Your Power is in Your Purpose

*K*nowing who you are and your purpose in life will stabilize you amid emotional storms. When people exit our lives, we lose ourselves. We make the mistake of attaching our value and purpose to other people. When that person walks out the door, they seem to take with them our very essence. This goes for our children as well. We tie our very being to them. That is why many people consider themselves a failure when others leave them. Going back to a prior point, people have agendas. Them walking out of your life does not diminish your value. If you are suffering from a decrease in value because a person left, that is a sure sign that you really do not know yourself very well or your purpose in life. You have not discovered your gifts and talents. When Tiger Woods, the famous golfer, went through his divorce, he was still a golfer. When he lost his endorsements, he was still a golfer. To this day, he is still playing golf. Another example presents itself in Pastor Paula White. Pastor White went through a huge public divorce from her first husband, but she didn't quit preaching. She was single for quite some time, but she was still a pastor. Then, years later, she remarried, but that didn't change that she was a pastor, either. She is still a pastor today, and none of the comings and goings of others in her life changed that. As you can see, no matter what, their gifts and talents remained. I strongly suggest to you to be sure you know yourself better than anybody else, other than God of course. Know what value you possess. Know what treasure is inside of you. You came out of the womb as a single individual with gifts and talents. Therefore, no one can take them from you. You are not a failure because of anyone else's presence or departure.

Golden Nugget #13
The Cost of People Pleasing

Some people feel like failures, because they have made a futile attempt at trying to please everybody while losing themselves in the process. This is a huge mistake. Accept the fact that you will not please everybody. Some of the decisions that you must make, some of the things that you must do, will not always please everybody. Many people feel loved when they are accepted by people. This goes back to the prior subject on self-love. Part of loving yourself means that you do not need other people's approval of you for you to be happy. You should approve of yourself. As long as you are doing what people want, people will applaud you. The minute you do not do what they want, many will turn their backs on you.

Remember, some love your fruit not your root. In other words, they love what you have to offer, not necessarily the person doing the offering. God deals with this all the time. I have learned to help people, not for the applause, but for a cause. I have learned to be consistent in my efforts, whether people think I'm doing a great job or not. I no longer perform for people, but for myself and God. I have learned that people are very fickle with their feelings towards me, and I believe the same holds true for you. Don't ever center your life around the acceptance of other people. One day, they'll be very loving towards you, but the next day things can change. So, find your center and always applaud yourself. Some of the most famous people in history, such as Mahatma Gandhi, Martin Luther King, Nelson Mandela and Jesus Christ, were not accepted by everyone. However, they continued in their cause, because the cause was more important than the applause. Find your cause, and you will not fall prey to the allure of the applause.

Golden Nugget #14

Avoid Their Negative Perspectives of You

This subject is one that we cannot bypass as unimportant. This matter directly impacts your mind. It can contaminate your perspective of success. It can influence your outlook on life in general. So, let's begin. "What they say or think about me is none of my business." I heard that statement one day while in church and found it to be very helpful in my life's journey. I now realize that people will always have opinions about me, be they positive or negative. So, why worry so much about what people think about me versus what I think about myself? It is an amazing freedom that happens in the mind once you are no longer subject to the opinions of others. We often say, "They said this or they said that," but we never stop to ask, "Who are they?" Why would I put so much credence on what they have to say, when sometimes I'm not sure who "they" are? And even if I did know who "they" were, what difference does it make when what they have to say about me is their personal opinion? And why keep negative people around me anyway? Think about it. Why would you have negative people around you who do not believe in you, don't support you, and always have bad things to say about you?

I believe that, in many cases, these types of people do not have anything good to say about you, because they still have not found anything good about themselves. As the bible says in Luke 6:45, "A good man out of the good treasure of his heart brings forth good; and an evil man out of the evil treasure of his heart brings forth evil. For out of the abundance of the heart his mouth speaks." How can they support you if they do not support themselves? Most of the people who are on the path to achieving something support one another. They do so because they are familiar with the struggles of trying to succeed. But onlookers, those who are sitting in the stands of life, hurl insults and criticize you. They do so, because it is easy to be a heckler of someone else rather than grind away at their own lost dreams. Have you ever watched a sporting event with a friend who always seems to have an opinion about what the team should have done? Meanwhile, you look at them knowing full well that if they were playing that sport, they could not perform even half of what they are demanding of the professional athletes. That is why they are watching and not being paid to play.

Opinions are freely tossed around from those who never do the grunt work to succeed. The only people who do not fit into this category are coaches and mentors. They are in your life to help you achieve your goals, not tear you down and discourage you. If you are around friends, family, or coworkers who are constantly talking negatively to you or about you, then the choice is yours whether to be around them or not. You decide who you want to spend time with. Surround yourself with positive people and get rid of the negative ones. On the other hand, if the negative person is your spouse, this requires a different strategy.

Quite often, spouses object to your vision for several possible reasons. One may be that they had plans of their own and feel like you are not supporting them. Having a strategy session at the kitchen table can help provide clarity. By discussing each of your goals, both of you will have a clearer picture of the game plan that will help each of you achieve success. Another common issue could be that your spouse may not be a visionary like you. Many couples are comprised of a dreamer and a person who simply wants stability and security. A clearly laid out plan can help to accomplish both goals. Explaining how you will be able to follow your dream without threatening the stability of the family will help in getting your spouse to feel more comfortable with your vision. This can go a long way in gaining their support during your quest for success. There may be other scenarios, but laying out a clear plan of action for them to see almost always works in your favor. I do not suggest separating or divorcing to accomplish a dream. Your dream should be for the good of you and your family, not just yourself.

But, what if those who do not support you are your parents or "programmers?" The term programmers refer to the people who may or may not have been your parents, but still had a hand in rearing you. Programmers include people who influenced you as you were growing up such as teachers, grand-parents, aunts, uncles, cousins, etc. You did not have the ability to choose them then, but you do now. If currently they are negatively impacting your life, you are going to have to implement a specific technique called deprogramming. Deprogramming simply means the rejecting of negative information. Many parents and programmers adopted a "virus" type of thinking long ago. They speak from an infected mind. Therefore, their programming does not have to be yours. Remember what we discussed earlier; what you believe to be true will always be true for you. What they say or have said is not always true. I am not against feedback for improvements, but putdowns and insults are unacceptable. Dr. Myles Munroe told a story of how one of his teachers called him an ignorant monkey and said that he could never learn anything. Dr. Munroe went on to obtain numerous doctorate degrees, along with several other degrees, and was one of the most notable speakers in the world in his day. As you can see, he chose not to accept the opinions of other people, including his teachers.

Finally, you must become a champion of your own thoughts. No one can control your mind except you. There have been many people throughout history who faced terrible circumstances, and yet their spirit was not broken. Their minds did not accept negativity as their final outcome. Never forget this statement, **"Advice is nice, but putdowns will be put out."**

Golden Nugget #15
Your Thoughts Control Your Success

There is another valuable lesson I learned through my ordeal that I feel is important to share with you. I now understand that my success will always be connected to the level of my thinking. Our minds act as the gas pedal to the vehicle called progress. The more our thoughts press forward in the relentless pursuit of a goal, the more our body and all our efforts will naturally flow in that direction. Likewise, if our minds release the pedal, all movement will slow down and eventually stop. Many of the endeavors I undertook, such as the childcare service, the various network marketing businesses, and so on, did not work out, because when I hit a bump in the road, I took my mind off the gas pedal causing the business itself to stop. That is why others were able to succeed while I sat feeling sorry for myself and calling myself a failure.

Let me give a better example. Years ago, when I lived in Oakland, California, I bought my first motorcycle. Having no formal knowledge of how to ride one, I fumbled around and eventually became efficient enough not to kill myself while riding it. One day, I was heading to church and came upon some train tracks. I approached with caution. I attempted to navigate the front wheel through the grooves of the tracks. Suddenly, I found myself on the ground in pain, having been thrown several feet from my new motorcycle. The bike itself was lying sideways in the middle of the street still running. My first thought, other than "Ouch," was, "What the heck happened?" I had slowed down and proceeded with caution, but still, the front wheel got trapped within the grooves of the tracks. Needless to say, I went to motorcycle school and obtained a proper education. In the course, they taught that when you are approaching train tracks, you must pick up your speed to avoid having your tires get caught in the grooves. I find the same to be true in life. How many times did I slow down when I should have sped up over the obstacles I was facing? No wonder I found myself depressed so often. No wonder I considered myself a failure. I slowed my mind down to assess every little obstacle to the point that I simply stopped the forward progress all together. There is nothing wrong with slowing down to assess interruptions to your forward progress. However, when you allow your mind to grind to a halt because of the challenges you are facing, that is a different scenario altogether. If we are to succeed at anything, we must be persistent in never giving up in our minds.

Golden Nugget #16

How to Turn Business Failures into Business Successes

*I*n my numerous attempts to succeed in the business world, I discovered that I had a talent that eventually made me successful. Most people call it "The Gift of Gab." For those who are not familiar with that term, it simply means that I am good at running my mouth. In the marketplace, I began to notice that I was a great salesman because that field requires great communication skills. That's well and fine, but I also discovered why I failed so often early in my career. Many organizations spend a lot of time and money on training employees how to implement different sales techniques to customers.

Millions of dollars are spent trying to figure out how to assist employees, sales agents, network marketing downlines, etc. in presenting their products or services. I take no issue with this as I believe it is a necessary expense, but there is a very important ingredient missing and that is emotional education. Over the past few years, individuals and business owners have asked me what caused me to rise from failure and become the top salesman in various organizations. Let me tell you a story to help shed light on my response to their question.

I vividly remember my experience at this particular job. I had decided to transition from a company where I was the top sales guy to this new company. You might be asking yourself why I made that unusual decision. If I was the tops sales guy, why leave? The answer is simple; the company had decided that they were no longer going to pay the sales team commissions. It makes no sense to hold the title of "Top Salesman" if there's no "Top Sales Pay." So, I came to the new company with guns blazing ready to become the king of sales. This company hired me because they had heard of my great reputation in the last company, so the stakes were high, but I felt confident that I would champion this challenge with ease. Boy was I wrong. I remember working there for the first three months with no sales. I went to all the trainings and all the meetings. I took great notes on the techniques they said would work to bring about massive sales. I would leave those meeting with enthusiasm and passion. I re-entered the real world ready to conquer using the golden strategies they said would work. My results? Failure after failure. The sales meetings continued. Now, I hated those meetings. I hated those meetings, because they would go through everyone's numbers one by one. I must admit that I envied the people who, when their name was called, would receive applause from everyone in the room for their success. Heck, that use to be me at the other company. So, you know what happened next? As the roster of names continue to be called, the applauses diminished. They diminished, because the next group of names were those who were under achievers. When your name was called, you felt like climbing underneath the table and pretending you'd lost a contact lens or something. A little advice, if you ever find yourself in this situation, two to three names before they call your name, pretend that you ate something foul. Run out of the room holding your stomach, and make a mad dash to the bathroom. I don't know why I never thought of that before. That would have saved me a ton of embarrassment.

I was the great salesman who couldn't sell a dog gone ice cube to someone in one-hundred-degree weather. I did not take my own advice of leaving the room. I sat in my chair angry, bitter, resentful, envious, and frustrated. I was failing again. I hated going to work. I dreaded even thinking about that place. Not because it was a bad place to work, but because it was hard to get motivated at a place that kept defeating me.

I remember the day that all of my emotions came crashing like a ship run aground. The company was a marketing agency that was a partner of Google.

So, the facility had a miniature play room to create a relaxed environment for the employees, just like Google's facilities. This room became my favorite place to hide from the torture chamber called "my desk." In the break room, they had a small indoor basketball hoop. I spent a lot of time with that hoop. It was my oasis. It was my mental vacation getaway. One day, I went to my oasis and no one was in there. It was just me and the hoop. As I was shooting baskets, I broke down and cried. **<u>Sales Leaders, Network Marketing Leaders, Company Executives, and any other leaders pay attention to what I am about to say here; this is important</u>**. Many of your employees are probably feeling the way I felt in that moment. As I was shooting hoops and crying my eyes out, a manager walked in. He was one of the toughest managers on the floor. I thought to myself, "Not only am I crying like a baby, but this particular manager had to be the one to walk in on me having a breakdown." He walked over to me, and he asked politely if he could join me in shooting hoops. What was I going to tell him, "No?" He's my manager! I sheepishly moved over a bit to share my oasis with him. He noticed my red eyes, but, for a moment, he acted like he hadn't and continued to shoot hoops and make small talk. I knew he'd seen my red eyes, but I played my role, continuing to ignore the elephant in the room. Until finally, he turned to me and asked how things were going. I know you, the reader, cannot see me at this moment as I write about this section of my life, but believe me when I say that I had to take a break. Even the memory of that day still brings tears to my eyes.

I turned to him and began to tell him the blatant truth. I told him how humiliating it was to have to keep coming into this place and failing day after day. I told him how much it hurt to go home to a loving wife who asked the dreaded question that no salesman wants to answer, "Did you make a sale today?" It cut at my pride to have to tell my beloved that, after three long months, nothing had changed. "No sale today." Of course, my angel would simply tell me that everything was going to be alright and to keep on trying, but my heart was screaming with pain, fear, and doubt. I had stopped believing in myself. I shared with him my daily routine of having to announce to my family that I had failed to make a sale again. This manager who was usually so tough, turned to me with understanding in his eyes and said, "One day, it's all going to click into place for you Patrick. Just hang in there. You got what it takes. Don't Give Up." "Oh great," I thought, "another rah-rah speech from a disconnected manager who really doesn't know how it feels to fail." But then, he began to open up to me about how many times he'd failed when he first started working at the company. He told of his emotional challenges and how he overcame them. He told me how many months it took him to make his first sale. He wanted me to know that he was not just trying to blow smoke up my behind, but that he really understood how I felt in that moment. He also wanted me to know that if I kept on trying I would succeed even as he did.

After divulging this top-secret information about himself to me, the sergeant-like manager walked out of the room and resumed his military-tough demeanor. I pondered on what he said and decided to take his advice. Not the advice of hanging in there and not giving up. I took the secret advice of how to fail like a champion, of how to manage my emotions. I finally understood that my feelings do not dictate my outcome. I simply have to outrun and outwork my emotions.

I began to work harder than ever before. Reports on who made the most calls for the day came in with Pat Murphy consistently being #1. No sales as of yet, but some success is better than none. Celebrate every success, no matter how small; today is just one step, but remember that in order to reach the top of any ladder, you must take one careful step at a time.

One special day, a client finally said yes. Finally, my first sale. I went home and celebrated with my angel. She was so proud of me, and I was proud of myself. Six months later, I won the company contest; I was the top inside salesman. My angel and I went on an all-inclusive, all-expense-paid vacation to Cancun Mexico on behalf of the company. What made the difference? The sergeant manager's willingness to share how he overcame failure. His willingness to open up about how he felt during those challenging times helped me recalibrate my emotions and remember who I was. I was the same top sales guy from the last company. I simply forgot how to win. I forgot that in order to win, you cannot depend solely on techniques. You must learn to win in the emotional arena as well. I appreciate him not speaking to me about sales techniques, because he knew I had those down pact. He recognized that I needed coaching in the area of handling my emotions.

Looking back on my many years in sales, whether it be in the business sector, the real estate industry, or the network marketing world, I consistently saw the same mistakes being made by the leadership team. They invested into techniques and not the managing of emotions. Mock trainings are one thing, but consistent rejection in the real world is another thing altogether. One must be taught how to handle failure and deal with it emotionally. The best way to do that is not by constantly showing off your prized staff members or by reinforcing how successful you were when you were in their shoes. No. It's done by talking about your failures. Spend time discussing how you felt when you were going through the same doubts and fears. Exposing your pain exposes your secrets to success. Don't tell me how it feels to be on the winning side; tell me how you managed to get through the losing seasons. If I learn how to navigate my way through failure, then success is mine just like it is yours.

Now, when I am asked to speak to employees, sales teams, or network marketing groups, I share with them my failures. Hiding my failures is hiding my success. They go hand in hand. You can't have one without the other. I come to where they are and walk their emotions to where I am. I don't sit across the emotional lake and yell to them to cross even though I know it's full of emotional sharks and crocodiles. I bring a boat over to their side and slowly bring them to my side of the lake. I become relatable. I create a bond. I do not push them faster than they are comfortable. I do not pretend to have amnesia when it comes to what I had to go through to become successful. **Pride serves no purpose as a team lead unless your team is a success.**

Later, that sergeant-like manager and I became great friends. I am thankful to him to this day. He became one of my best sales mentors. I no longer saw him as a mean, tough manager. I understood what made him tough. His willingness to unveil his battle scars created a brotherhood. I no longer feared him as others did. I respected him. One day his truck was having problems, and I was able to assist him in getting it fixed. He paid it forward, and the favor was returned.

Golden Nugget #17

The God Factor for Success

I purposely left this section for last. Whether you are a person of faith or not, I strongly believe that we are all affected by our connection or disconnection from our Creator. Disconnection from God is disconnection from self. I have grown to believe that we all came from somewhere and from a higher power. I refer to this higher power as God. And if God is our source, how could we possibly achieve our highest and best use of our life if we are disconnected from the One who created us in the first place? This is why I believe many people feel like failures. Disconnection from God is disconnection from the vital nutrients that your mind, body and soul needs to function at an optimal level. Even if you have it all, but are disconnected from the Source, you may have a feeling that something is missing in your life. How many famous people do you know who are still suffering unhappiness, even though they seem to have it all? When I say all, I mean all that this world has to offer like money and fame.

I believe this discontentment with life stems from, what I call, "the God factor." You can achieve everything and still feel like you have nothing. But if you have the God factor and an understanding of your purpose in life, I believe you will be a truly happy person. You do not have to be rich to be happy, but you do need to be connected to God to find true happiness and contentment. Could it be possible that you are feeling like a failure, no matter how much success others think you have, because of your disconnection with God? I know a lot of people who go to church and claim to know God; they may act like God is their best bud, but closer examination of their hearts reveals that there may be some distance between them and God. Begin to work on closing this gap as I had to do, and you may find the peace you seek. In Philippians 4:7 it says, "And the peace of God which transcends all understanding, will guard your hearts and your minds in Christ Jesus."

Another important reason I feel we all need to reconnect with our Creator is to find out why we were created in the first place. Not knowing this can certainly bring feelings of failure and depression right to our front door. Could it be possible that you are pursuing goals that have nothing to do with why you were sent here to Earth in the first place? For an example, I have a fish tank in my office. What if the fish decide they no longer wish to live in water? What if they climb out of the tank and start flapping about on the floor? Although they have accomplished their goal of leaving the water, they are still unhappy, because now, they cannot breathe and they will die a slow death. Why? Because they are living outside of their element. They are trying to succeed in an environment that they were not created for. Could this be true for you as it was for me? When I seriously asked God to help me understand myself, He introduced me to the real me. Not the me I thought I should be because everyone else liked me that way; I rediscovered and fell in love with the me that I buried a long time ago. I found that my gift was talking and running my mouth. Looking back on my past, going all the way back to grade school, I use to get in trouble for talking too much in class. I have always been a great communicator, but I was using my gift for the wrong reasons. I was using it to get attention and to entertain and please everyone else, rather than myself and my Creator.

So, my gift was always there. I simply did not see it as a gift, because talking was so natural for me. In fact, when I lived in California, I use to speak before large audiences at church. While many people get what is called "stage fright" when speaking in front of large crowds, I am the very opposite. The larger the crowd, the more comfortable I feel. Why am I like that? Because I was designed to be that way. What were you designed to do that you may be ignoring? I am no longer living in frustration and failure, because I tapped into the reservoir of my gift. It fits my personality. It was always there; I just needed my Creator to show me what I had and how to use it. I never would have thought that I would be the author of several books, but here I am, the new Pat Murphy. I like this new me. I feel natural. I do not have to pretend anymore. I no longer stand on the stage of people pleasing. I now perform for only one, my Creator. Finally, I am free. Thank you God for introducing me to myself.

Could it be possible, that this is the reason why you feel like you're failing at the things that you are attempting to do? Being disconnected from God will have you on a roller coaster, attempting to try things that may not be a good fit for you.

Another point to make here, is the fact that some of you may be angry with God just as I was. That is equivalent to a person with a broken iPhone saying that they no longer want to be in any discussions with Apple, yet they still desire to have their phone fixed. Please do not make the same mistake as I did. I thought that God was not paying attention to me and that he had abandoned me in my plight. It was simply my thinking process and emotions that clouded my judgment. The Bible says that He will never leave you nor forsake you, even unto the end of this world. I now know that to be true, and I thank Him for that. Even when I turned my back on Him, He never turned His back on me. He was kind enough to introduce me to the true meaning of love, and I hope the same happens

for you. Peace and blessings to you, and thank you for
reading this book.

About the Author

Patrick Murphy is an author, speaker, and Certified Life Coach that specializes in relationship coaching. He is also an anti-divorce advocate and a former real estate investor and radio talk show host.

The abrupt end of his marriage of 27 years brought with it an emotional breakdown that, for a time, left Patrick feeling lost and worthless, but it also brought the knowledge and drive needed to support others experiencing the same devastating pain. Patrick's profound teachings have helped countless people around the globe improve their relationships. However, he longs to help even more. He's vowed to touch the lives of 55 million people before he leaves this world, and he hopes this book will help him reach that goal.

Patrick also established The Conflicts of Life organization. The COL aids individuals with relationship conflicts, and under Patrick's leadership, has grown from a radio show with no listeners to a multi-media marvel that's reached over a half a million people through broadcasts, public speaking events, and social media. The COL Facebook page has reached a following of more than a quarter million, a feat Patrick is very proud of.

Today, Patrick is happily remarried to Nancy, his "Green Tea Angel," who is the love and backbone of his life. Together, they find fulfillment through helping others.

Patrick Murphy
CEO of The Conflicts of Life

For more information, please visit our website at www.theconflictsoflife.org

or our Facebook page with over 270,000 followers at **The Conflicts of Life**.

For Speaking engagements and guest **appearances** a

Email: info@theconflictsoflife.org

E-Home: **Theconflictsoflite.org**

Author's Recommended Books